Prehistoric Beasts UNCOVERED

The Titanosaurs
Earth-Shaking Dinosaurs

By Dougal Dixon

Ruby Tuesday Books

Published in 2018 by Ruby Tuesday Books Ltd.

Copyright © 2018 Ruby Tuesday Books Ltd.

Editors: Ruth Owen and Mark Sachner
Designer: Emma Randall
Production: John Lingham

Image Credits:
2010 Vila et al: 20 (bottom); 2013 Vila et al: 29; 2014 Vidal et al: 14 (bottom); 2015 Knoll et al: 28 (bottom right); 2016 Martinez et al: 18 (top), 26; Alamy: 10 (bottom), 10—11, 21 (bottom), 27 (right); Creative Commons: 16 (bottom); Getty Images: 22—23; Tyler Keillor: 23 (bottom); James Kuether: Cover, 4—5, 6—7, 8 (bottom), 9, 12 (top), 14—15, 17 (top), 17 (bottom), 18—19 (bottom), 20—21, 31; Kenneth Lacovara: 24—25; Public Domain: Shinobu Ishigaki 12 (bottom); Kristina Curry Rogers: 28 (bottom left); Ruby Tuesday Books: 13; Shutterstock: 2—3, 8 (top), 11 (bottom), 13, 15 (bottom), 16 (top), 18 (centre), 19 (top), 19 (centre), 27 (left), 28 (top).

British Library Cataloguing In Publication Data (CIP) is available for this title.

ISBN: 978-1-911341-76-5

Printed in Poland by L&C Printing Group

www.rubytuesdaybooks.com

Contents

Naming Dinosaurs

All living things have a **Latin** scientific name in two parts – a **genus** name and a **species** name. You are *Homo sapiens*. A dog is *Canis familiaris*. It is the same with dinosaurs – for example, *Triceratops horridus* and *Tyrannosaurus rex*. Some of the titanosaurs featured in this book are named *Patagotitan mayorum*, *Dreadnoughtus schrani* and *Saltasaurus loricatus*. When we talk about these dinosaurs in the book we will only use their genus name.

The name titanosaurs comes from the Titans, who were god-like beings in ancient Greek myths.

The shadows of tall coniferous trees stretch out across a hot, dry plain.

Another slow-moving, giant shadow creeps across the land. It is created by a creature as tall as the trees.

A giant foot, as big as a tree stump, crashes down into the dusty soil.

This is *Dreadnoughtus.*

It is one of the biggest land animals that ever lived.

And it is a titanosaur.

The Land of the Giants

The giant dinosaur shares its home with other *Dreadnoughtus* and a herd of *Saltasaurus*.

Saltasaurus are also titanosaurs. They are smaller than *Dreadnoughtus*, but have the same long necks, long tails and elephant-like body. The *Saltasaurus* also have a covering of armour on their backs.

A New Generation

As the *Saltasaurus* herd moves off, it leaves behind patches of disturbed ground, dotted with white speckles. The female *Saltasaurus* have been laying eggs. Thousands of round eggs lie in shallow scrapes in the ground, ready to be **incubated** by the hot sun.

The next **generation** of earth-shaking titanosaurs will soon hatch.

Saltasaurus

Dreadnoughtus

Saltasaurus nest

The Earth-Shakers

Dreadnoughtus and *Saltasaurus* lived about 70 million years ago in the late **Cretaceous period**. Their **fossils** have been found in the part of the world that is now Argentina, in South America.

The Biggest Dinosaurs

Even the giants started small. About 230 million years ago, before the colossal titanosaurs walked the Earth, the main plant-eating animals were a group of sheep-sized, long-necked dinosaurs called sauropodomorphs.

Anchisaurus

Anchisaurus was a sauropodomorph. It could walk on its back legs and use its front feet as hands. However, it spent most of its time on all fours, to support the weight of its plump body.

When: 195 million years ago
Where: North America

Long and Low

In time, the sauropodomorphs developed into the dinosaur group called the **sauropods**. And they became BIG! Some sauropods, the diplodocids, were long and low.

Diplodocus

Diplodocus, with its long, whip-like tail, is the best-known of the diplodocids. One species, *Diplodocus hallorum*, was about 32 metres long – almost the length of two buses.

When: 152 million years ago
Where: North America

Standing Tall

Other sauropods were tall, carrying their tiny heads at great heights. These animals are known as the macronarians.

Giraffatitan

Giraffatitan was a macronarian with long front legs that made its shoulders very high. Its long neck allowed it to feed from the tallest trees.

When: 145 million years ago
Where: Africa

Adult *Giraffatitan*

Young *Giraffatitan*

The New Giants

The diplodocids and macronarians died out in the early Cretaceous period. Their places were taken by the titanosaurs, such as *Dreadnoughtus*, *Patagotitan* and *Saltasaurus*. These giants **evolved** from the macronarians and were the most massive animals that ever lived. As of 2018, about 50 species of titanosaurs have been discovered.

Meet a Titanosaur

A titanosaur had a big body, a long neck and tail, a small head and four strong, thick legs.

The Biggest Titanosaur?

In 2014, **palaeontologists** in Argentina discovered a new species of titanosaur. They named it *Patagotitan mayorum* and they believe it could be the biggest animal to ever live on land. Around 130 bones were **excavated** from six different skeletons. Using these fossils, scientists estimated that *Patagotitan* could grow to be 37 metres long.

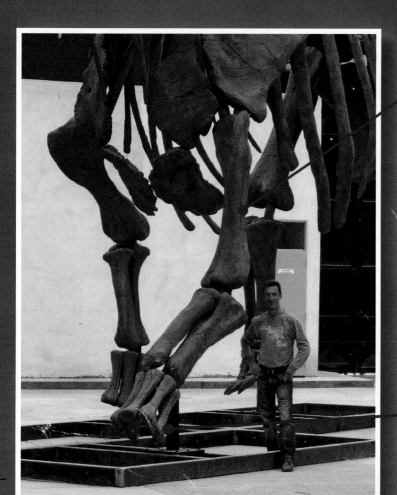

FRONT LEGS
Unlike most four-legged dinosaurs, a titanosaur's front legs were the same length or longer than its back legs.

FRONT FEET
A titanosaur's front feet had no toes, just vertical bones in a horseshoe shape.

SPINE
Usually in sauropods the sections of the spine are tightly linked together to give strength. The sections of a titanosaur's spine are quite loosely joined. This suggests that a titanosaur's back was more flexible, perhaps for bending and stretching while feeding.

HIPS AND SHOULDERS
A titanosaur's hips are narrower than its broad shoulders. This can be seen in titanosaur tracks where the impressions of the back feet are closer together than the front feet.

This is a reconstruction, or life-size model, of *Patagotitan*'s skeleton. The model is based on *Patagotitan* fossils and bones from other titanosaurs.

BACK LEGS
The upper bone in the back leg is longer than the lower bone. This is always a sign of a slow-moving animal – for example, modern hippos have this type of arrangement.

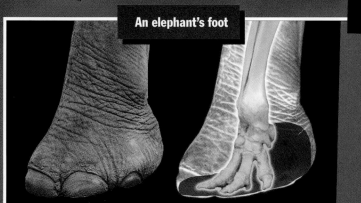

An elephant's foot

Feet Like an Elephant

A titanosaur's back feet were probably arranged in a similar way to an elephant's. The toes sloped down to the ground, and to spread the weight, it probably had a thick cushion of gristle beneath its foot. Scientists can't be sure of this, however, because unlike bone that fossilises, gristle quickly rots away after death.

The Size of the Giants

A complete adult titanosaur skeleton has never been found. But scientists have uncovered plenty of individual bones. From these finds, they are pretty certain that the titanosaurs were the biggest land animals that ever lived.

Why Did They Grow So Big?

The titanosaurs' great size may have enabled them to gather food at heights that other plant-eaters couldn't reach. Maybe their size was a defence against predators.

Are We Asking the Right Question?

Maybe we should ask: Why are modern animals, like elephants, not so big? A **warm-blooded** mammal such as an elephant needs a lot of food so its **metabolism** can produce enough energy. If it grew to the size of a titanosaur, there would not be enough hours each day for it to eat the huge quantities of food it would need. Perhaps the titanosaurs grew so big because they had metabolisms that allowed them to exist on smaller amounts of food.

Palaeontologist Professor Shinobu Ishigaki alongside the titanosaur print

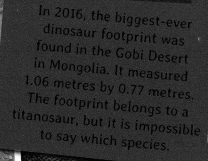

Big Foot

In 2016, the biggest-ever dinosaur footprint was found in the Gobi Desert in Mongolia. It measured 1.06 metres by 0.77 metres. The footprint belongs to a titanosaur, but it is impossible to say which species.

The Biggest Dinosaur That Ever Lived

When a new species of titanosaur is discovered, news reports often claim it's the biggest dinosaur that ever lived! The problem is that we can never be completely sure of the length of the complete animal.

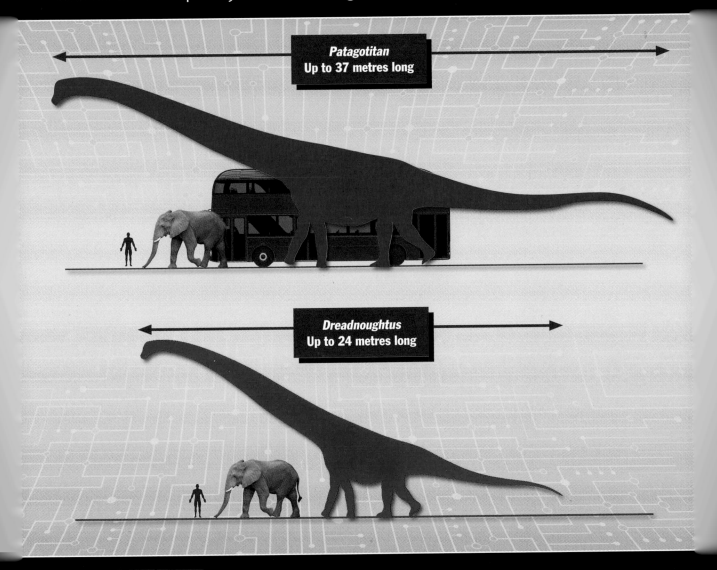

Patagotitan
Up to 37 metres long

Dreadnoughtus
Up to 24 metres long

Big Numbers

Usually, parts of a titanosaur's spine, especially the end of the tail, are missing. Also, when the animal was alive, the sections of its spine would have been separated by fat and pads of gristle. Without knowing how thick these were, we cannot know the true length of the living titanosaur. All scientists can do is estimate a dinosaur's size using the available fossils — and often scientists disagree with each other!

Giants with Armour

In the 1970s, palaeontologists got a surprise when a titanosaur with armour was discovered in South America. Why would a big animal like a titanosaur need to be armoured?

Meet *Saltasaurus*

The armoured animal was found in the Salta province of Argentina, so it was named *Saltasaurus*. Its back had a covering of tiny rounded or five-sided scales, just a few millimetres wide. Embedded in the scales were bony oval plates called osteoderms. Spikes grew from the osteoderms.

Spiked osteoderms

Tiny, tough scales

Fossil osteoderms

The side view of an osteoderm

The osteoderms are up to 12 centimetres long.

How Was the Armour Arranged?

It's likely the spikes were arranged in rows, but for now, scientists don't know. The osteoderms have only been found lying loose among other fossilised bones, not attached to anything.

The Armoured Titanosaurs

Not all titanosaurs had armour. From the discoveries made so far, scientists think about a quarter of titanosaurs, the smaller species, were armoured.

How Big Was Saltasaurus?

Scientists have estimated that Saltasaurus grew up to 8 metres long and probably weighed less than an adult elephant.

Why Have Armour?

Compared with the truly armoured dinosaurs, such as ankylosaurs, *Saltasaurus*'s armour was fairly light. So maybe it wasn't used for defence. The backbone of a titanosaur was not as rigid as the spines of other sauropods. Perhaps the armour was there to stiffen its back, like a crab's shell. A baby's bony osteoderms were solid, but adult ones were hollow. Maybe they were a store of **calcium** that young animals used to help their bones grow.

An ankylosaur called *Gargoyleosaurus*

World of the Giants

Titanosaur fossils have been found in many parts of the world, but they mostly lived on the southern continents. Their enormous bones have been found in South America, Africa, Madagascar, India, Australia and New Zealand.

A Long Walk

Savannasaurus was a big titanosaur that lived in Australia 93 million years ago. Its ancestors were from South America. They reached Australia by **migrating** across Antarctica. In the late Cretaceous period these three great landmasses were joined together and formed a super continent called Gondwana.

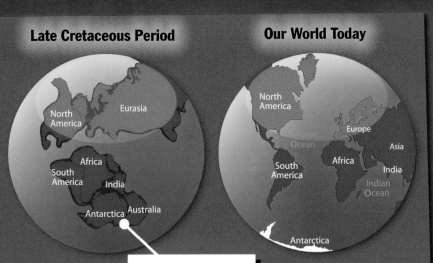

Late Cretaceous Period

North America
Eurasia
Africa
South America
India
Antarctica Australia

Our World Today

North America
Europe
Atlantic Ocean
Asia
South America
Africa
India
Indian Ocean
Antarctica

The supercontinent of Gondwana

A New Titanosaur Species?

When a titanosaur skeleton is found, palaeontologists must decide if it's a completely new species. They carefully study the bones to look for tiny differences in size and shape. It's like looking at the bones of a lion and a tiger. Both animals belong to the cat family, but their skeletons have many differences. It's the same with the bones of different titanosaurs.

As of 2018, only one incomplete *Savannasaurus* skeleton has been found. This diagram shows where the bones fitted in the animal's body.

The Giants Return to North America

For most of the Cretaceous period there were no sauropods in North America. Then, in the late Cretaceous period, a land bridge formed that connected North and South America. A titanosaur called *Alamosaurus* migrated north from South America and spread throughout western North America.

A herd of *Alamosaurus* migrating north

Did a Beast Called *Titanosaurus* Exist?

The name *Titanosaurus* was given to some sauropod fossils found in India in 1877. Since then many sauropod bones have been called *Titanosaurus* fossils because they could not be identified as anything else. This makes the name *Titanosaurus* a "wastebasket taxon". The name is used, like a rubbish bin, for all the fossil bits that are still a mystery. The name *Titanosaurus* will never be used to name an actual dinosaur.

Dwarf Titanosaurs

There were actually some little titanosaurs, too. *Magyarosaurus* was about the size of a pony. It lived in the part of Europe that is now Romania. During the late Cretaceous period Europe was covered in a shallow sea dotted with islands. Small, or dwarf, versions of animals often evolve on islands because there is less food available.

A *Magyarosaurus*

A Big Vegetarian

We know that titanosaurs were plant-eaters. But did they use their long necks to reach leaves and twigs high up in trees? Or did they sweep their necks low to feed on the plants at their feet?

High Feeder? Low Feeder?

When we look at the angle of a titanosaur's neck and head, it looks as if it fed on high branches. If we examine the scratches on a titanosaur's teeth, they show that it fed on tough, gritty food, such as ferns and cycads. These were plants that grew near the ground. Maybe titanosaurs ate high and low. This is something that scientists still have to prove.

The teeth of a titanosaur named *Sarmientosaurus*

A cycad plant

Futalognkosaurus was a titanosaur that lived in Argentina about 87 million years ago.

Prehistoric Poo Proves It!

Chunks of fossilised poo called **coprolites** can show what food passed through a dinosaur – 66 million years ago! When scientists found a titanosaur coprolite in India, they discovered it contained bits of conifers, cycads and palm trees. The big surprise was that it also contained grass seeds. Scientists thought that grass plants did not evolve until after the dinosaurs died out. Now a piece of prehistoric poo has shown us that grass was around in the late Cretaceous period.

A dinosaur coprolite

Did Titanosaurs Eat Rocks?

Scientists have found stomach stones, known as gastroliths, inside titanosaurs. Plant-eating birds swallow stones to help grind up food in their stomachs. Scientists thought that dinosaurs did the same. Now, new **research** has shown that titanosaurs did not swallow enough stones to help with digestion. The latest thinking is that they swallowed stones as a way to get calcium, which they couldn't get from plants.

Gastroliths, or stomach stones

Fossilised Nests

Imagine a wide, flat **river plain**. The land is dotted with dinosaur nests, full of eggs just ready to hatch. Then imagine that the river bursts its banks, flooding the plain and burying the nests under mud.

Thousands of Eggs

This is exactly what happened around 80 million years ago at Auca Mahuevo in Argentina. In the late 1990s, a team of palaeontologists, led by Luis Chiappe, made an incredible find — around 400 dinosaur nests and thousands of fossilised eggs!

No Mums Required

There are no signs of the parents at the site. The female dinosaurs must have laid their eggs and moved on. This suggests that the babies were able to take care of themselves as soon as they hatched.

Dug by Dinosaurs

Each nest was a scrape in the sand. The sweep of the scrape shows that it was made by the back feet of an adult dinosaur. The eggs were not buried. We can tell this because the fossil eggs were covered by a layer of rock. The rock formed from the mud that was deposited by the flood.

Good Luck for Science

The flood was bad luck for the titanosaurs, but good luck for science. The disaster gave us a perfectly fossilised nesting site that has allowed scientists to discover so much about the early life of titanosaurs.

This illustration shows how the nests must have looked.

The eggs were almost round and up to 15 centimetres in diameter.

Each nest contained 15 to 40 eggs.

Fossilised Baby Dinosaurs

Inside the eggs, scientists found fossilised **embryos**, or unhatched baby dinosaurs. From the teeth and the shape of the skull bones, they identified the babies as titanosaurs. The embryos even had skin with armoured scales. This shows that they were babies of an armoured titanosaur, such as *Saltasaurus*.

A model of a baby *Saltasaurus* inside its egg

A Baby Titanosaur

Kristi Curry Rogers is a palaeontologist who studies titanosaurs. She is an expert in a titanosaur named *Rapetosaurus*.

Meet *Rapetosaurus*

Rapetosaurus lived in Madagascar around 70 million years ago. Its existence was announced to the world in 2001, after a skeleton of a juvenile animal was discovered. It was 8 metres long. It's estimated an adult could grow to about 15 metres long.

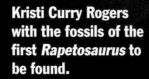

Kristi Curry Rogers with the fossils of the first *Rapetosaurus* to be found.

An Incredible Discovery

In 2012, Kristi was working at the State University of New York. In a drawer filled with fossils from Madagascar, she discovered some tiny bones. The bones had been in storage for more than 10 years and no one had spotted what they were. Kristi realised she'd found something very special — the bones of a baby *Rapetosaurus*.

A New View of the Titanosaurs

Scientists knew what titanosaur embryos looked like. They also knew what juvenile titanosaurs were like. But no one had ever seen a very young baby before.

A Miniature Adult

Most animals change their shape as they grow. This is because babies usually behave differently from adults. Perhaps they scamper around instead of moving slowly. These differences can be seen in the animals' skeletons.

This wasn't the case with the baby *Rapetosaurus*. Its tiny, fossilised bones were the same shape as those of a juvenile or a giant adult. This tells us that baby titanosaurs must have walked and behaved just like the adults.

This juvenile *Rapetosaurus* stood 2.5 m tall at its hips.

A Tiny Titan

Kristi and her research team studied the tiny dinosaur bones that were found in the drawer. They learned that the baby was between 39 and 77 days old when it died. They estimated the baby weighed about 3.4 kilograms when it hatched. At the time it died, it weighed about 40 kilograms.

Kristi stands with a life-size model of the baby *Rapetosaurus*.

Uncovering Titanosaurs

Most of the titanosaurs that have been discovered were just a few fossilised bones. Sometimes, however, palaeontologists get lucky!

Finding *Dreadnoughtus*

In 2005, palaeontologist Kenneth Lacovara and his team discovered *Dreadnoughtus*. The team uncovered a single tooth and 145 bones from a site in Argentina. The fossilised bones came from two animals and made up about 45 percent of a whole skeleton.

Kenneth Lacovara at the *Dreadnoughtus* dig site

Fossils are wrapped in plaster to protect them

Dreadnoughtus's tail

A Huge Excavation

The animals died between 84 and 66 million years ago. They were probably drowned and buried quickly under mud when a river burst its banks. The fossil find was so big it took four years to excavate.

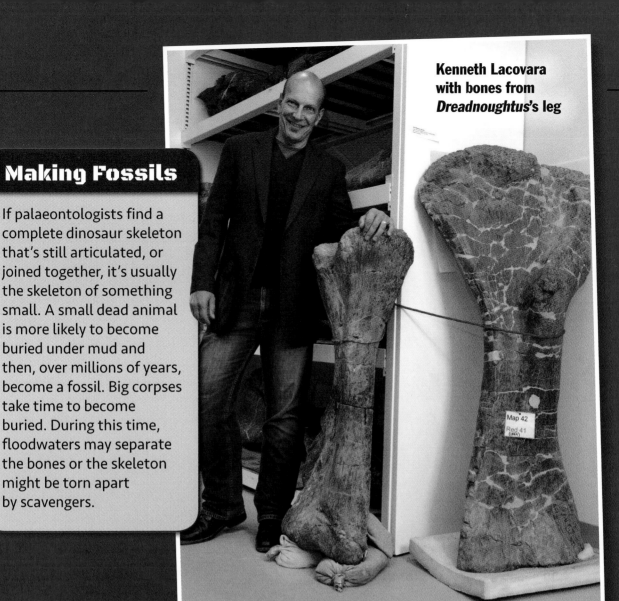

Kenneth Lacovara with bones from *Dreadnoughtus*'s leg

Making Fossils

If palaeontologists find a complete dinosaur skeleton that's still articulated, or joined together, it's usually the skeleton of something small. A small dead animal is more likely to become buried under mud and then, over millions of years, become a fossil. Big corpses take time to become buried. During this time, floodwaters may separate the bones or the skeleton might be torn apart by scavengers.

Rebuilding *Dreadnoughtus*

Many bones come in pairs. For example, if scientists find a left shoulder blade, they can assume the right shoulder blade will look the same. Based on this, it was possible to build up an accurate picture of around 70 percent of *Dreadnoughtus*'s skeleton.

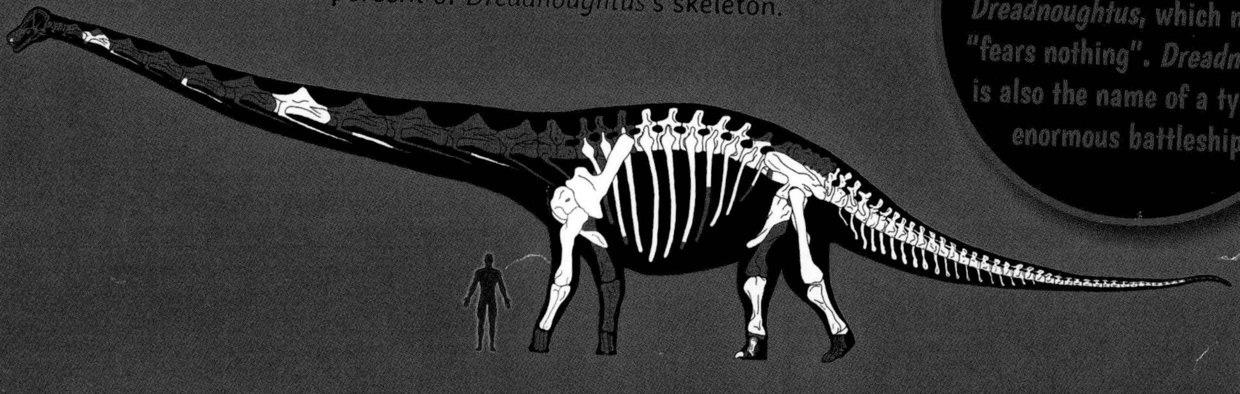

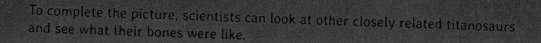

To complete the picture, scientists can look at other closely related titanosaurs and see what their bones were like.

Fears Nothing

Kenneth named the dinosaur *Dreadnoughtus*, which means "fears nothing". *Dreadnought* is also the name of a type of enormous battleship.

Into the Lab

Once a dinosaur skeleton is excavated it is taken to a **laboratory** where scientists work away to uncover its secrets.

A Head Start

A dinosaur skull is usually made of delicate pieces of bone. It is the first thing that falls to pieces when a dinosaur dies. In 1997, a very rare complete titanosaur skull was found in Argentina. The skull belonged to a *Sarmientosaurus*. It told us lots about the head shape of the titanosaurs. By looking at how the head joined to the neck, we can tell it held its snout downwards. This could mean it fed on low-growing plants.

The eye sockets are large, so it had big eyes. Was *Sarmientosaurus* active at night?

The position of the ear canals show that it communicated by low grunts and rumbles. Sounds like this carry over the ground. This also shows that the head was held low.

Testing Eggs

It's possible to work out the body temperature of a dinosaur by examining the **atoms** that make up its eggshell. Scientists developed this technique using modern birds and their eggs. By testing titanosaur eggshells, they've learned that titanosaurs seem to have had higher body temperatures than humans.

How Heavy Were the Titanosaurs?

It is very difficult to measure the weight of a dinosaur that has been dead for 100 million years. So how do scientists estimate a titanosaur's weight?

Patagotitan's back leg

Method 1:

Measure the diameter of the leg bones from a modern animal and how much weight the bones carry. Then measure the diameter of a dinosaur's leg bones and work out how much weight could be carried by bones of this size. These calculations give us a weight of about 32 tonnes.

Method 2:

Make a model of the dinosaur, measure its volume and then scale up the volume to life size. Volume is the amount of space that an object fills. Then measure the density of a living animal, such as an elephant. Finally, multiply the density of the living animal by the volume of the dinosaur.

For a titanosaur this can give a weight of between 32 tonnes and 80 tonnes – a big difference! Also, we can't know that the model was an accurate shape or that a dinosaur's muscles, fat and insides were the same density as an elephant's.

Titanosaur Tech

When palaeontologist Kristi Curry Rogers wanted to learn more about a baby *Rapetosaurus*'s bones, she used a CT scanner (computed tomography scanner). This machine takes X-rays of an object, such as a bone, to create a detailed 3D picture of what's inside.

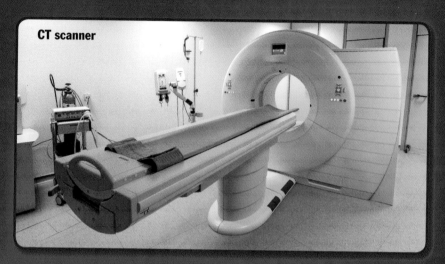

CT scanner

Inside a baby *Rapetosaurus*

Kristi was able to see the growth line in the baby's leg bone. This shows when an animal hatched from its egg. From this piece of **evidence** Kristi could work out that it only lived for a few weeks. It was also possible to see that the baby grew quickly compared with other animals. Kristi also discovered that the cartilage, the gristly material, between the baby's bones had stopped growing. From studying modern animals, scientists know this means the baby dinosaur starved to death.

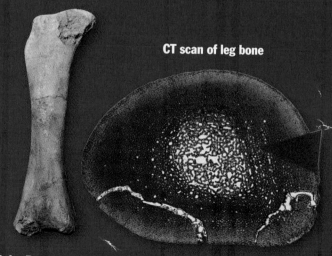

CT scan of leg bone

Baby *Rapetosaurus* leg bone

The red arrow shows the growth line.

Big Body, Tiny Brain

A CT scanner can produce pictures of empty spaces as well as solid bones. A dinosaur's brain rotted away, but the empty space where it sat remains inside the fossilised skull. A CT scanner can produce a 3D image of this space that shows us the size and shape of a dinosaur's brain.

An adult titanosaur's brain

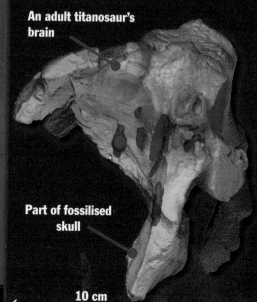

Part of fossilised skull

10 cm

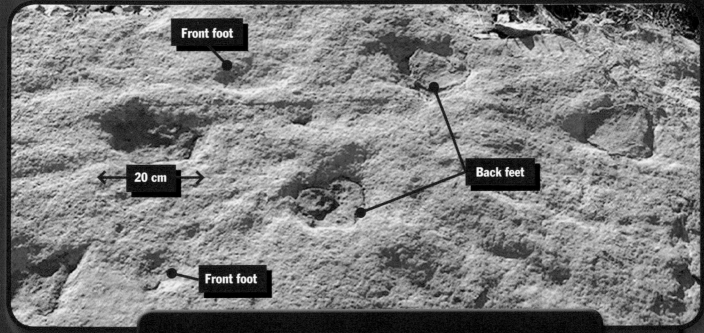

Front foot

Back feet

20 cm

Front foot

Shedding Light on Footprints

In Spain, palaeontologists uncovered a trackway of titanosaur footprints. To accurately measure the tracks, they used a technique called LiDAR (Light imaging, Detection and Ranging). LiDAR measures the surface of the ground by bouncing laser beams off it. The data was used to work out the walking speed and stride length of the animals.

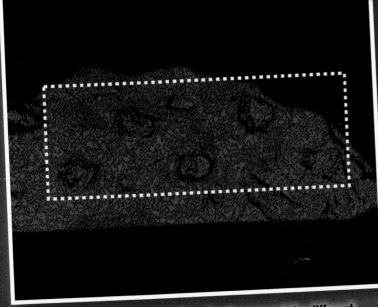

The different colours on a LiDAR read-out represent the different heights of the footprints and the surrounding ground.

Don't Jump to Conclusions!

One trackway in Spain shows the tracks of two different sizes of titanosaur. The set of footprints made by the smaller animal show that it was walking in exactly the same way as the larger animal. Does this evidence tell us that young titanosaurs walked like adults? Or were the smaller footprints made by a different species of titanosaur altogether? We can't say for sure — yet.

Glossary

atom
The smallest particle of an element. Atoms are the building blocks of every substance.

calcium
An element that is important in the structure of bones and eggshells.

coprolite
Fossilised animal dung. Coprolites are useful to palaeontologists — they tell what a fossil animal has been eating and how it digested its food.

Cretaceous period
A period in time that came between the Jurassic period and the Paleogene period. It lasted from 145.5 million years ago to 66 million years ago. The Cretaceous period was the end of the Age of Dinosaurs.

embryo
An unborn or unhatched baby.

evidence
Information that can be used to show that something is true. For example, coprolites show what types of plants were eaten by titanosaurs.

evolve
To change or develop slowly, often over a long period of time.

excavate
To dig into the ground to uncover something, such as a fossil.

fossil
The hard remains of a living thing that are preserved in rock.

generation
A group of animals or people born around the same time.

genus
A classification of living things. A genus may cover several species. For example, the genus *Panthera* includes *Panthera leo*, the lion, and *Panthera tigris*, the tiger.

gristle
A natural tough, bendy substance that pads out the junctions between bones. The proper name for gristle is cartilage.

incubate
To keep eggs warm so the babies inside can grow and hatch.

juvenile
A youngster. A person or an animal that has passed the childhood stage and is not yet an adult.

laboratory
A room or building where there is equipment that can be used to carry out experiments and other scientific studies.

Latin
A language that began in ancient Rome. Scientists still use Latin today when naming animals, plants and other living things.

metabolism
The working chemical processes of a living body, including breathing and digestion.

migrate
To move from one place to another and then back again in order to find food and mates, or to avoid extreme weather conditions.

palaeontologist
A scientist who studies animals and plants from the past.

research
Information that is gathered and studied in order to prove facts.

river plain
The flat land on either side of a river that may be flooded from time to time.

sauropod
A member of the group of plant-eating dinosaurs that are four footed and have long necks and tails, and small heads. The name means "lizard foot" because the scientists who first studied them thought that the foot bones were arranged like those of a lizard.

species
Different types of living things. The members of an animal species look alike and can produce young together.

warm-blooded
In an animal, able to keep the body temperature at more or less the same level whatever the temperature of the conditions around it.

Index

Learn More Online
Could you be a scientist uncovering the buried secrets of prehistoric beasts?
Go to: www.rubytuesdaybooks.com/dinosaurs